Born in Dallas, reared and raised in the suburb of Farmers Branch, Mark Brookshire has his roots deeply anchored in the great state of Texas, walking and working his way through the labyrinth of life, all the while, writing and collecting his thoughts along his varied path.

He tried his hand on numerous trades: deckhand on oil rig, painter, construction worker, cable guy, etc. Creating not a working-class hero. To the contrary, no hero, no glamor, only a toughened hide and a man of many skills – part Handyman/part Renaissance man.

Winning a poetry contest at college, then writing for a prospective cartoon that was mismanaged to failure, were some of his early writing ventures. Still, it simmered inside until it finally boiled over in a contemplative heap of thoughts and incites. Now, with great earnest, it must proceed. Heated emanations from the soul!!! To be continued…

To my son Michael, family, and real friends.

Mark H. Brookshire

THROWN OUT OF EDEN

RHYMES OF/AND REFLECTION

AUSTIN MACAULEY PUBLISHERS™
LONDON • CAMBRIDGE • NEW YORK • SHARJAH

Ordering Information
Quantity sales: Special discounts are available on quantity purchases by corporations, associations, and others. For details, contact the publisher at the address below.

Publisher's Cataloging-in-Publication data
Brookshire, Mark H.
Thrown Out of Eden

ISBN 9781649794246 (Paperback)
ISBN 9781649794253 (Hardback)
ISBN 9781649794260 (ePub e-book)

Library of Congress Control Number: 2023919745

www.austinmacauley.com/us

First Published 2024
Austin Macauley Publishers LLC
40 Wall Street, 33rd Floor, Suite 3302
New York, NY 10005
USA

mail-usa@austinmacauley.com
+1 (646) 5125767

The Inferno Within

Where tragedy sleeps, nightmares are hidden.
Where doors are locked, access is forbidden.
Such a house, constructed upon lies and deceit.
Will burn from within, conflagration complete.

Secrets of shame, hidden in the dark.
When revealed, the necessary spark.
Dysfunction burns the family crest like coal.
The fire, one of arson, out of control.

A raging tumult, mighty and fierce.
Glowing sabre, the family armor, it will pierce.
Now, a house without windows and doors.
Incinerating, the heat index soars.

Hope of escape, so often contemplated.
Overwhelmed by reality, then deflated.
Its' inhabitants who lived to betray and conceal.
Their casket, the space within. <u>Funereal.</u>

The Greatest Man: Nobody

Somewhere, sanctuary hides a man you know nothing
about.
But be assured, his power runs deep and devout.
He misses nothing, senses keen.
Immeasurable, value unseen.

Of nothing in this world does he obsess.
He seeks not to enslave, nor to possess.
Prestige and payment suit not his needs.
With honor and dignity his daily deeds.

Rank and reward are of no appeal.
Status and station he need not reveal.

This man? You shall never know his name.
He of little fortune, void of fame.

His deeds, simple, gallant.
Never boasting, secure in his talent.
Neither soldier of fortune nor white knight.
His agenda, peace, gentility, day and night.

Someday, you may feel an unmistakable presence.
Not of this world, not of the flesh, but of his essence!

Cold, Blue, Obsession

Gun control; a juxtaposed contradiction.
Two words men cling to with such conviction.
Weapon of mass murder, instrument of insanity.
Its' legacy? A blackened scar, disfiguring humanity.

Through the ages, the gun, so fabled.
Leaving behind, the killed, the disabled.
Often falling into the hands of the deranged.
Body counts rise, statistics have not changed.

Coveted and craved by thugs and losers.
Allowable, by law, to maniacs and abusers.
Like a bullet entering the head.
Brain permeated, by the power of lead.

Science, intellect, nor gentility can hold it back.
As always, available, the gun, on the attack.
Built only, to divide, conquer and kill.
Prescribed daily dosage, his bitterest pill.

The day man ceased to think and feel.
Was the day he created cold, blue, steel!

Be thee prince, be thee pauper, the bullet knows not...of
what is proper.

Man Mythological

Who will levitate to be today's: "Man Mythological"?
Modern-day Helios. Cosmic. He, astrological.
Abdicating not his stardom, nor renouncing his gift.
Each day with chariot, evening gloom to lift.
Revealing the dawn, exposing the beauty.
Relishing with fire his appointed duty.

Vapidity to he, embodies grief.
Statuesque, rigid, in self-belief.
Opposing this enemy as if the Grim Reaper.
The beacon of life. The Torch Keeper.
Spurning today's purveyors of doubt.
Smashing, with hammer to anvil clout.

Distant relics. Forgotten. Eons behind.
Disarmed. By the power of mind.
For those bound to such ordinary stations.
He has neither the time, nor the patience.

Soaring. Questioning. Gods beseeched.
Loftier ambitions. Altitudes reached.
Like Jason, who slayed the serpents seven.
Born to Zeus, to inhabit his heaven.
Destined to solve all things cryptic.
Gaze the constellations. The Moon ecliptic.

(Quatrain)

Misunderstood. At war with the uncertain.

Never, ever, frightened.

Incredulous. Pulling back the curtain.

Legend. Titan. The Enlightened!

The Truest Man

When there is uncertainty, where there is fright.
When there is darkness, he is the light.
In times of plenty, if he must be without.
No time for self-pity, no time for self-doubt.

As always, doing the best he can.
Answering the challenge. He is the truest man.
To rise above, over and beyond.
He need not possess a magic wand.
The power within, an immeasurable force.
His soul follows his chartered course.

Wary of the chaos, yet he does not flee.
The makings of a coward. Not he.
The trek, never easy, never paved.
The thrill, the journey, one to be craved.
Never waver, never cower.
This is his finest hour.

Simply the man nature intended.
Best foot forward, excellence extended.
He <u>must</u> venture into the arena. Face the unknown.
Courage exists to the very bone.
Standing strong, yet bending with the breeze.
He looks in the mirror; he likes what he sees.

While the timid start to crumble and fall.
Like a statue, he always stands tall.
To these convictions, he remains loyal.
The weak are peasants. He is the royal!

The 4 Horsemen Ride; Apocalypse Wide

The 4 Horsemen and their trusty steeds.
Unwavering agents of appointed deeds.
Doling out prophecy with biblical passion.
Mounted horses. White, red, black and ashen.
Each vigilant in assigned earthly patrol.
Scripture's deadly virtues they obediently extol.

The 1st Horseman at the Lord's behest.
Horse of white. He, of conquest.
Adorned with the Victor's crown.
Conquering soldier, repute renown.
To others, pestilence and disease.
Malarial monster. A swarm of fleas.
At the ready with bow and arrow.
Inflictor. Infection into the marrow.

The 2nd Horseman with the greatest of swords.
Deity designate. To enflame the hordes.
Rider of insurrection and dread.
A mount of blood-fire red.
Empires fall. Death tolls soar.
Master of mayhem. Master of war.

The concept peace, of <u>no</u> worth.
Divesting harmony from the face of the earth.

The 3rd Horseman. Horse of black.
Deadly shade of plunder and sack.
Unbalanced scales. Weight of starvation.
His gift to God, the sickly; his oblation.
The poor, the famished, his only focus.
Destroying fields. Swarms of locusts.
Iron scepter. No mortal need.
In his wake, crops of noxious weed.

The 4th Horseman; keeper of the corpse.
Hades astride his colorless horse.
His scythe leaves the scar of the beast.
No more Suns to rise in the East.
Grim Reaper. Servant of death.
Fumigating flocks. Apocalyptic breath.
Messenger, heartless, of no valor.
Sculptor of headstones. Mausoleums of pallor.

Man, below deck. Nothing more than human storage.
Oarsmen in bondage. Rowing. Endless voyage.
These Masters casting plagues with wanton hand.
Laying waste to mortal earth. Orb of windswept sand.

Lost Soul. Amongst the Clouds

Directionless. Migration unknown.
Windswept avian. Off course. Alone.

Flustered. Blustered. A frail canary.
Cast to the sky. No aviary.

No guidance. No bearing.
No compass. Sun glaring.

No sanctuary. Tempests accost.
Dizzying heights. Forever lost.

A metaphor. Wayward being.
Searching. Yet never seeing.

Featherless. Falling groundward.
Losing altitude. Spiraling downward.

Crashing sorrow that will never cease.
No place of calm. No ebb. No peace.

A Concept Beyond

Could memory ever fully save.
The sheer ecstasy of a crashing wave.
Hear the rocks echo Neptune's roar.
Waves disappear, to retrieve many more.

The sea, mother nature's original child.
Full of beauty, born limitless and wild.
A foreshadowing of wonders to be.
She had more in store than the crystal sea.
More, much, much more, was she to bear.
Reward. Endless marvel for all to share.

A concept so free of bleakness.
Nature's beauty is its uniqueness.
Seasonal script, we can always depend.
Perfectly written, beginning to end.
Boundless, it knows not of direction.
Allegory that is perfection.

For this, man, a being blessed.
Fortunate, though unjustifiable, guest.
Lowest valley to the highest peak.
You will find beauty. If beauty you seek.
Eternally constant, despite constant abuse.
Pictorial delight. Subtle tones. Vivid hues.

Nature exposes life, sometimes death.
The gentle breeze, the eternal breath.
The wind a language for all to hear.
The voice ceaseless, gentle or severe.
The hurricane's howl, the evergreen's swaying chant.
Touching the eminent redwood to the frailest plant.

A day will come, man's final chapter, drawing to a close.
The bitter end, he so ruthlessly chose.
When his fate is sealed, his continuance denied.
The last heart has ceased, the last sob has been cried.
The unworthy occupants of earth have withered and died.
Nature shall be eternally exalted and deservedly so.
With an unpolluted breeze and a virgin snow.

Funeral Through a Fence

A sibilant snow covers all with its silken shroud.

As another soul is laid to rest in a necropolis proud.

A solemn moment to discuss God and fate.

The deceased is then lowered to lie in state.

For those remaining, the routine of worry now returns.

I am struck by their inevitable concerns.

For those laid to rest, no further demands.

They've done their best, it's out of their hands.

Accepting reward of eternal tranquility.

A peaceful solitude. True nobility.

Theirs is the ultimate truth, they live only in spirit.

They've come upon death and no longer must fear it.

Death. Unwelcome. At My Door

Shroud hovering. Impending gloom.
Over me, shadows. Vultures loom.
Soaring. Ominous. Prophets of doom.

Limbs shiver. Chilled to the bone.
Crippling dread. Fear of the unknown.
Solitude. Decaying. Abandoned. Alone.

Hounded. Imprisoned. Isolation.
Chained. Abandoned. Desolation.
Combined, a wretched conflation.

Left nothing, but a knowing fear.
Images, not of earthen tones, but sheer.
Path before me, unobstructed. Clear.

Not kindness. A blindness. Never restored.
Subjected. Neglected. Not of accord.
Recompense nil. Final reward.

Specters. I thought I'd never live to see.
Realities. I thought that never could be.
Brutal. Final. They finish me!

Questions? Afterlife?

When fate denies me future breath.
Resignation to inevitable death.
To end the days of sweat and toil.
To toss away this human coil.

Free at last, from the ties that bind.
Released, unburdened of the daily grind.
Past transgression? I cannot erase it.
Penalty? Reward? I will face it.

Onward to realms unknown, doubted.
One so feared. One so touted.
To which haven anointed?
One of freedom? Or exile appointed?
Depot Hell or gilded station?
Cursed perdition? Gifted salvation?

Existing on high, amongst the clouds?
Wallowing below Satan's darkened shrouds?
Ceaseless burden? Lasting leisure?
Abrupt sentence of misery? Endless pleasure?

No fear, a curiosity, of what lies ahead.
Ambivalence. Uncertainty. Without dread.
Of the banality Earth, I've had my fill.
Into the afterlife! Of my own free will!

May I Rest in Peace

Atheist. Such a meaningless label.
To those who question religious fable.
Tired scripture of the power and the glory.
Man's creation. Imaginative story.

Justifying acts of misguided evil.
Dating back to time medieval.
Haven; for those prone to deceive.
Intolerance; for those who dare not believe.

Handed down by evangelical phonies.
High-income, unregulated, untaxed cronies.
Worn out pages. Yellowed theology.
Unfulfilled verses. Pure mythology.

Just another wives' tale at the very essence.
By now, to the point of obsolescence.
Monk-like chants. Incessant humming.
Still waiting for the Second Coming.

(Quatrain)
Each of us a sinner; the Devil's pawn.
Sanctimonious sermons; such a bore.
Wake me when it's over. (Stifling a yawn).
Please forgive me…if I snore. (ZZZZ)

The Devil's Embodiment...Prejudice

When born into the primeval wild.
You, as I, were only a child.
Of the concept of color, we were both unaware.
It mattered not, who was dark or fair.

But soon to be noticed was black and white.
Which stood for darkness? Which stood for light?
At that fateful time, it was decided.
It was easier to hate, than to be united.

Forgotten, were moments of true accord.
When kindness was given without motive or reward.
From that day forward, tragically afflicted.
Our own self-hatred, misdirected.

Wretched malignancy, a worldwide tumor.
Fueled by self-preservation and unfound rumor.
Prejudice thrived, a posterity of weakness.
Shrouding each race with an imposed bleakness.

Horrid legacy of hatred and spite.
Symptom of our own inner blight.
As powerful as any nuclear blast.
This the dye to which we were cast.

Shadows of ignorance will spell the end.
Can we find a way to halt this sickening trend?
Let us not be bound by anger without basis.
Beyond the tinted façade of people's faces.

Once and for all, we must bury prejudice. Lest we'll be consumed.
It must be interred…Never to be exhumed!

The Power of Persistence

The path to greatness is landmarked with errors, as is the road to ruin.

The road to ruin paved only for the stubborn and short-sighted.

Rendered temporary when mistakes are acknowledged, and wrongs are righted.

Mistakes are compounded by ignorance and denial.

Admit the wrongdoing, but never hold trial.

Dwell not on things never to be undone.

But, labor long for the good yet to be done.

True talent, a self-reliant nature, one can never extract.

Submit to the cause. Let the cause be exact.

Know when to advise. Know when to consult.

A favorable balance will bring a favorable result.

It matters not how greatness is perceived.

It matters only, if greatness is achieved.

Do not be tormented by the standards of others.

It's your dream, so have your druthers.

"Persistence is the true measure of faith in oneself."

Disease. Intolerance

A man gets older he holds tight to a grudge.
Each year easier to harshly judge.
Anger-hardened arteries, he won't forgive.
Blood flow a trickle, strained by a sieve.
Atrophy tightens the grip. Arthritic fingers.
Resentment residual, it hovers, it lingers.

Allowed to fester and infect.
Debilitating effect.
Victim of self-capture.
Denied salvation. Denied rapture.
Malady of bitterness will age him.
Enslave, enrage and encage him

Animus devours from within.
Though the offense, forgivable sin.
Handcuffed by blind disdain.
Only he, can remove ball and chain.
Attitude, so self-provincial.
Depth of wound, inconsequential.

With maturity, he comes to realize.
Irreparable harm to those who despise.
For true reconciliation, atonement and kindness must align.
As the Bard famously penned: "To forgive is divine!"

Defeat. Complete.

This era of men. Silent. Stoic.
In a time so damned non-heroic.
Where men eke out a meager existence.
A trivial, stifling, subsistence.

Conformity of daily convention.
Over-industrialized. Without invention.
Patents of thought rarely created.
Uninterested. So easily satiated.

Sunrise of morning twilight.
Sunset. Lacking twilight.
Moon shone down on nightly plight.
No rescue. No mounted white knight.

Headstones of similarity.
Vestiges of only familiarity.
Loss of zeal. Of no appeal.
Mummified. Unable to feel.

The senses slowly dwindle.
Internal flame to rekindle?
The slightest flicker left?
To this era of: "Men bereft".

Woefully Lacking.
Woefully Short

Perfection applies only to ideals.
Pursuers ill-equipped. Human nature reveals.

Inept beings. Dreamers.
Procrastinating schemers.

Mortal challenges never come near.
Pitifully short. The evidence clear.

Dutifully unfit. Never approaching.
Paragons safe. None encroaching.

Commonplace. The extent.
Ordinary. Simply relent.

Sapience of the greatest mind.
Left in the dust. Far behind.

It is Nirvana. Not of the earth.
Man attempts. It is mirth.

The human void. Not of perfection.
Broken mirror. Shattered reflection!

Diary of a Revelation

I look back at the guy I used to be.
A void of emptiness is all I see.
With an outlook so mindless and slanted.
Taking everything and everyone for granted.
An existence inane, incomplete.
Reveling in my own deceit.
Carrying a sickness, seeking no cure.
No direction. Ranks of the unsure.

Judging one and all by the surface.
Life without cause, life without purpose.
Devoid of love, devoid of trust.
Driven by fear, driven by lust.
Cool on the outside, inside I would burn.
Always taking, never giving in return.
Each acquaintance, a fleeting story.
Never a moment of being sorry.
An animal that finds itself caged.
Within the bars, the battle raged.

Insecurity rears its ugly head in many ways.
Confusing. An endless maze.
A man is not a man unless he knows the fear.
His day of reckoning is drawing near.
While never lonely, yet always alone.

With regrets, my past I atone.
So blind. Did I not know?
In the mirror stood my only foe.

Deep down I really knew.
To thyself one is often untrue.
Can one truly amend.
With words from a solitary pen.
I ask not to be exempt.
This day, I will at least attempt.
In lieu of apologies, I make these vows.
Make the most of the future and what it allows.

Today's mirror reflects the image of a changing soul.
A soul come to grips with things neglected.
Who wants only to respect and be respected.

Destroy. Create Not, Demons

Cast a leery eye.
To the ebony sky.
If you let him intrude.
He, you will not elude.
Dreams, he will besmirch.
Isolate you, in the lurch.

He is master of the hounds.
Making his nightly rounds.
Man-eater. The menace spreads.
Serenity, torn completely to shreds.
Demonic depth of badness.
Beyond the mortal madness.

Blood-curdling. Evil. Rabid.
Nightmares, he will inhabit.
Like the curse of the vampire.
Darkness. His evening empire.
The reaper of fright.
Keeper of the night.

Terror at the basest level.
Your soul, he will bedevil.
Haunting the midnight hour.
Sanctity, he will devour.

Your being, your aura, chilled.
Stay inside, lest you be killed.
Alas, you have the power to destroy.
Power within, to deploy.
He is but self-imposed machination.
Manifestation of the imagination.
There is no boogeyman, no ghoul.
Create him. You are the fool!

Waste Ye Not. Fortune Begot

The power of intellect cannot be measured.
Omniscience inherent, gift to be treasured.
So many mishandle this rarest of talents.
Minimum withdrawals from a limitless balance.

Malfeasance. Equal to money laundered.
Like the addicted gambler, riches squandered.
Could man witness a more tragic waste?
Than intelligence misused, intelligence misplaced.

The brain's economy at the brink of depression.
Knowingly bankrupt. Cerebral recession.
Licensed thievery of one's very wits.
Detonated by ignorance. Blown to bits!

I'm a Dreamer, Too

Come join us, occupants of the distant mist.
Surrealistic members scratched from reality's list.

Fantasy is our borderless realm.
Climb aboard and take the helm.

Willing inmates of innocence, we remove lifelong guilt.
By destroying the Gothic-strong past and all it has built.

Doctors of fancy. Life transparent, never vague.
We are the cure…Life is the plague.

Inquiry of Love

The inquiry of love occurs so often.
Remaining a puzzle from crib to coffin.
Existing in the emotional collage.
To some it is real, others, a mirage.
Truly a concept sublime.
Pursued since the beginning of time.

Said to be the cure-all of mankind.
Admonished by some. Left behind.
Never meant for those who deceive.
Realized only by those who believe.

Love is what keeps you alive.
They who have it, they shall thrive.
Those with doubts, a life of grief.
Hate robbing them, like a thief.
Love can be a savior to all.
Answering even the loneliest call.
Whom never asks for love, I wish they understood.
Within love, lies the ultimate good.

Love is the extinction of lies.
Love eliminates desperate cries.
Love is all and all it seems.
Love gives hope. Love gives dreams.

Love's expanse is always secure.
Love is heaven pure.
Love is ceaseless. Sheds all refrain.
Love warms. Then cools like the rain.
Love is affronting, never concealed.
Like flowers beautify the field.
Love is fruitful. Vast in its domain.
If love exists, man shall remain.

Somewhere Forgotten

Given to moments of introspection, I often wonder.
How many loves and friendships time has put asunder?
Look what time does to a once reliant shoulder.
Hasn't time made you and I a little colder?
Time can heal, yet time can endanger.
Yesterday's friend becomes today's stranger.

While romanticizing moments of flower-faded past.
Did I really think those days would forever last?
On occasion, I wistfully recall that face with no name.
How could you just forget me or am I to blame?
Wasn't it just yesterday that I first met you?
Then how did I let myself just forget you?

I think of you, ambivalence reigns.
Contentment. Accompanied by heartfelt pains.
You're not the first to fade into the oblivious haze.
A thousand tomorrows erase a thousand yesterdays.
The bonds and trusts have appeared and died.
Victims to mistrust and hollow pride.
Time is as subtle as time itself. Relentless to a fault.
Grinding ever faster, until brought to a halt.

To scrapbooked recollections, I must hold fast.
I want such moments to last and last.

I refuse to sever ties.
Deny myself the final good-byes.
Each instant, fleeting it may have been.
Reminders of the pleasure that is a friend.

Wax nostalgic and always remember.
Be it years ago, or some December.
Set aside quiet reflection as much as you please.
Hearts are molded by memories such as these.

(Quatrain)
Perhaps a far away friend is thinking of you this very day.
Or will remember you some solitary night.
Joyous in knowing somewhere you are thought of in a very special way.
Forgetting the distance time has reared. Everything will be alright.

Seek Ye Forever

The languid lovers in somber repose.

> Smugly dream as they begin to doze.
> Even now they dream of the perfect mate.
> With little wonder their minds are opiate.
> Add their names to the list.
> Dreaming of perfection, while perfection is missed.

> Men and women paint such pretty pictures.
> Mr. or Mrs. Right remain lifetime fixtures.
> Find someone special, they continue the search.
> Seeming content being left in the lurch.
> Intuition, they no longer trust.
> Subtle hunger becomes a driving lust

> To a man, what be a woman? To a woman, what be
> a man?
> She of fair face or he of strong hand?
> In terms, of a simple meeting.
> One hello, the heart takes a beating.

> Even in moments of doubt.
> Somehow, they remain devout.
> Though the differences a bit abstract.
> Sometimes, opposites really do attract.

Through the maze, they still pursue.
To think of it, the thing to do.
Though beings of intelligence, it is nature inbred.
To seek a companion, to warm their bed.

Men and women, together and apart.
For the future, the motto should impart:
"Sometimes we love, sometimes we hate.

A revelation, something cosmic, something great."

My Dreams. Others' Schemes

I slumber. Barely dormant.
My dreams. Ceaseless torment.
Friends arrive from the past's mosaic.
Labeling me obsolete and prosaic.
Cruel, spiteful beings, unrelenting.
Constant, vengeful ghouls, unrepenting.
Strangers as well, join the fray.
Confronting. Unforgiving display.

Combining forces, creating tumult.
Vicious fiends of heartless insult.
They persecute. Condemn. Venomous vent.
I emerge defeated, totally spent.
No reason or substantiation, at the attack.
Some face to face. Some at my back.
My nocturnal armor, they wittingly pierce.
A Freudian tragedy. Wild. Fierce.

Nightly punishment of tease and taunt.
My visions, they continue to haunt.
A peaceful soul, without crime.
Must I be victim in this nocturnal time?
Women leery. Mistrusting. Zealous.
Men despising. Pugilistic. Jealous.
Swords, words, hacking. Wounds deep.

Foes. Warriors. Bastardize my sleep.
Bloodletting demons. Blades unsheathed.
Cosmic clouds, a foulness breathed.

Hypnos, god of sleep. Won't you spare me?
Morpheus, god of dreams. Must you ensnare me?
Though I of sin, I do not sin every day.
Nightly punishments. Won't you allay?
Release me from my nocturnal chain.
I am forgiving. You embody disdain.
Sending the infernal Harpies to pester my sanity.
I remain humble. You are vanity.
At last, daybreak brings this drama's finality.
Awake. I destroy you with dawn's reality!

An Eye for an Eye.
A Death for a Death

How do we deal with the murderous among us?
The walking, stalking, human fungus.
Nightmarish assassins. Surreptitiously, they creep.
Into our sacred domains. A liquid, they seep.
Animalistic. Savage. No self-control.
Devoid of conscience. Devoid of soul.

Mindless beasts. Though born to reason.
Helpless. Given to heartless acts of treason.
Destroy, dismember, discard. Not a trace of sympathy.
Without feelings. Nor a thought to empathy.

When captured, they must pay for such insanity.
Feel the torture(s) of their inhumanity.
This pestilence deserves no rehabilitation.
Experience the wrath. The same debilitation.
They deserve not, another breath.
Entitled, as they perpetrated. To an agonizing death!!

Ode to Mistrust

I've gazed at the once friendly tide, its waters nearing
drought.
Felt the foot of injustice, as it kicks us about.
Witnessed faces taught with anger, lined by stress.
Reluctant. Carrying on, nonetheless.
Your strength is dwindling and so is mine.
But where does one finally draw the line?

What crime? To be stripped to the very limb.
Our dignity removed by some unseen whim.
This world and its dreadful sobriety.
Speaks volumes of our so-called society.
Commentary on such a place could never expose.
The stifling effect running rampant in its throes.

What could one possibly obtain?
What things are of merit in the realm humane?
All I see is a lack of sincerity.
What little exists, is indeed a rarity.

From this day forward, my space, do not endanger.
An arms' length allowance for you, fair stranger.
I trust you sense my upright sanity.
Today, I am as faceless as humanity.

Just as the light fights the shadows of night.
Another soul has faded, completely out of sight.

In Whom Can You Trust?

When your flag of identity is completely unfurled.
True self revealed to the rest of the world.
When it's well known what's truly on your mind.
That time of maturity, you will find.

There are four kinds of humanity.
Testing your sacred sense of sanity.
Two types that like and dislike you for the <u>wrong</u> reasons!
The other two that like and dislike you for the <u>right</u> reasons!

The first pair weigh you down with lies and strife.
The second pair lift you up and enrich your life.
The former, of no concern.
From the latter, you may learn.

Hypocrites will come and go by the dozens.
True friends, true enemies, keep as close as cousins.

Some Respected.
Some Neglected

Some view the elderly with a sense of pride.
Others deem them disposable, to be cast aside.
Some find them a source of inspiration.
Others look for a date of expiration.
Some defer to grandmother and grandfather.
To others, they're just a bother.

Though they stoop. Though they age.
In their own right. Each a sage.
Perhaps bed ridden, infirmed.
Their wisdom, confirmed.
Experience. Something to give.
Artistic collage to relive.

Remember each, an enduring tale.
Be a sponge, absorbing detail.
Give attention, put them on file.
Each, of inimitable style.

Someday memory will fade.
No cards to be played.
Deserving of utmost respect,
Not youthful, selfish neglect.

To do so is to be cursed.
Someday, the roles reversed.
Give admiration. Rise above.
Give them time. Give them love.

Self-Construction of Self-Destruction

Never blame fate. Though it manipulates.
Man falls prey, when he capitulates.
Bad karma, an easy scapegoat.
Buy a ticket. Take a seat. Aboard the <u>hate</u> boat.

Complain, criticize, recuse all they like.
Useless. A finger in the dike.
Mumble, stumble, grumble as they wish.
A plate served. A ptomaine dish.

Seated together, a band of accusers.
Table reserved. Born losers.
Thespians of over-dramatization.
Inflicted. Self-victimization.
Practice chosen. They employ.
Weapon within. Ready to deploy.

Dripping slowly. Bottomless funnel.
No exit. Endless tunnel.
Affliction. Festering inside.
Their choice. Their suicide!

Power! Belief in Oneself

I care not, of those who know nothing about me.
Yet I relish, in disproving they who doubt me.

Bothered not, with the trite, the mundane.
Of no consequence. I will not entertain.

Such inanity, I let not endanger.
Of no importance. It is a stranger.

Knee-deep in epiphany. Discoveries abound.
I seek the joy of thoughts profound.

The realm of depth is where I exist.
Haven. Where revelations persist.

When I see it. I will know it.
I am pundit. I am poet.

For I am the power. The glory. Forever and ever.
The seeker. The thinker. To forever endeavor.
…(Amen).

Born Free.
(To) Remain Free

Has man engaged in a more shameful activity?
Than his legacy of wild animals in captivity.
What worse act of evil could he possibly do?
Than enslaving nature's children in a public zoo!

Beasts within four walls. Birds in a cage.
Each filled with resentment and inner rage.
Metaphor of amputated legs and clipped wings.
Making them puppets, complete with strings.

Animal lovers, we hear them prattle.
Yet they ride atop them, in the saddle.
We work them. They should work us.
Trained and chained. In a circus?

They obey, without a voice.
While we are granted a choice.
To unbridle, unlock, unleash. Forever release.
Unchained, unshamed, untamed. To do as they please!

Be an animal lover, but always from afar.
When we invade, we only frighten and mar.
View them with awe in their natural state.
Never by enticing or luring with bait.

Omnipotence. When allowed to live in the wild.
Abused. When domesticated, trapped or beguiled!

The True "King" of Beasts

Allegory of majesty from tail to mane.
King. Zenith of nature's food chain.
Color of Africa, unmistakable brown.
Cape buffalo, giraffe, he will take it down.
Equipped with only tooth and claw.
Fearsome predator. The symbol of awe.

Pure nobility flows through his being.
Always on the attack, never fleeing.
Stalking the jungle or open ground.
His quarry, until satiated, he will hound.
If a rival challenges, he will fight.
It is his nature. It is his right.

From his instinctual duties, he will not run.
Asking no quarter, giving none.
Sentry on guard, far and wide.
Protector, patriarch, of his pride.
Be he aged warrior. Be he young and spry.
To keep this position, he will die.

Man should be so unflinching, so willing.
Without weapon, to do his killing.
Technology enables the courage to ravage.
The lion, master. He, the savage.

We should have such honor and dignity.
In its stead, we exude dishonor and enmity.
He kills for nourishment, strictly survival.
Man kills for sport or jealousy of rival.
Killing to the brink of the lions' extinction.
Shameful legacy, a wretched distinction.
We are primitive. Our logic overturned.
We ignorant animals. While he has learned.
When history records the damage done.
We will have lost. He will have won!

A Crime Revisited

He came to this city amid much apprehension and applause.
But with time, Dallas had come to respect its new champion
to the cause.
To show this new respect they appeared that day in mass.
To welcome the new frontier and its leader, every color and
class.

Yet on that day the menace to man, the ugly assassin lay in
wait.
To dash the hopes of millions in his fickle instant of hate.

With the plottings of man and the ensuing violence.
Dallas was quickly shamed into an embarrassed silence.
Helped along by the media and a petulant persecution.
It endured the guilty verdict by some vague prosecution.

For decades Dallas has sought forgiveness, never pity.
Is that too much to ask for a people and their city?

It is time for this metropolis to climb up from its painful
descent.
To forgive itself as an unfortunate, yet random setting for
such a tragic event.
The human frailties exposed that dreadful November.
Lest we forget, we will always remember…

"As for the future, faith in our principles we must fully entrust.

For the acts of a savage few will never indict the good, nor punish the just."

Deposed Despot of Danger

Modern-day Mephistopheles.
Tragedian. Sophocles.

Accelerant. Lighting the fire.
Born to disrupt. Born to conspire.

Conflagrant. Stoker of the flame.
Accuser. Master of blame.

Speeches. Caustic, spiteful.
Rhetoric, inciteful.

Behavior, outrageous.
Diseased. Contagious.

Malignant condition.
Acts of sedition.

Castle chaos. He is Lord.
Lunatic fringe. Umbilical cord.

Ambassador of hatred.
Nothing off-limits. Nothing sacred

Self-proclaimed hierarchy.
Purveyor of anarchy.

Disruptor. Dislodger.
Veteran Draft dodger.

Cult leader in public.
Creator. Banana Republic.

Narcissistic squire.
Revolutionary liar.

Call him not, Sir Donald.
A clown. Ronald McDonald.

Legend cemented.
President Demented!!

Much Ado About No One

Charles Manson, may we never, ever, again hear the name.
Not another, bloody word of his nefarious fame.
Back in '71, we heard his prison door slam.
After that, why did anyone give a damn?

Five-foot-tall, dirty vermin, weaselly skunk.
I'd have liked five minutes with that little punk.
Hippies and media enthralled with this loser, this loner.
Why was this bum glorified to cult-like persona?

Human refuse. Simple white trash.
Never earning a single dollar of legitimate cash.
Nothing to remember. Nothing to commemorate.
Let him reside in hell and conflagrate!

For those wretched beasts who did his calling.
Enjoy a future of mid-earth falling.
Hades is waiting, a place reserved.
A hot seat with the devil, so deserved.

Forget forgiveness. Forget parole.
You forfeited that, along with your soul.
At long last, may they and their story die.
Bid them an eternal, a heartfelt and happy goodbye.

Sentence of prolonged death, justified.

Like your victims, slowly crucified.

Forever may you wallow in your moribund pain.

And may your names, never, ever, be mentioned again!

Mitochondria of Hypochondria

The hysteria; Hypochondria, can only diminish.
Deplete, devour, destroy, then finish.
Psychosomatic affliction.
Suffocating restriction.
Betrayed. Enabled. Delusion-predicated.
Poisoned. Sickened. Society self-medicated.

Of its own inception.
A crutch of deception.
Creating a world fraught with agitation.
Damaged. Warped imagination.

Themselves, never recused.
Absolved. Never the accused.
Excuses create swirling confluence.
Dizzied. Absorbing every influence.

The mirror reveals the source.
Captains of their chartered course.
Lost. No sense of direction.
Capable of, complete resurrection.
They refuse, interred by gloom.
Dead. Buried. Resigned to the tomb.

True illness? Never revealed.
Debilitating madness. Neatly concealed.
Walking symptoms of their very own.
Brittle. Ossified. To the very bone.
Edifice built by their own deceit.
Obliterated. Destruction complete!

Unholy Martyrs? Holy Wars?

A man's religion does not define him.
Deemed liberating, it will only confine him.
Enslave, ensnare, slowly entwine him.

Theories. Fairy tales. Obsolete.
Scriptures. Untruths. Odes of deceit.
Fruition. Fulfillment. Incomplete.

Justification. Biblical. Condoning Holy Wars.
Betrayal of Commandments. Settling scores.
Espousing abstract verse, as body count soars.

Interpretations skewed. Absolving misdeed.
Hypocrites. Priestly. Meeting denominational need.
Safely sanctified cathedrals, as soldiers bleed.

Jerusalem. Vatican. Regardless the city.
Without qualm. Not a trace of pity.
Stained-glass windows, oh so pretty.

Protected pitch men. At their worst.
Gifted oratory, so well-versed.
If there is an afterlife. May you be cursed!

Messiahs? Pariahs

The unshorn herd following the Judas goat.
Jumping blindly aboard a leaky boat.
Branch Davidians, the People's Temple, Heaven's Gate.
Brainwashed zombies in a catatonic state.
Led by comical Messiahs of sexual perversion.
Twisted scriptures of religious subversion.

Giving away their worldly goods and bank accounts.
Every possession. Every dollar. Regardless the amounts.
Falling victim to self-treason.
No dignity or semblance of reason.

Pity them not. Puppets. Fools.
Dutifully drowning. Ever-rising pools.
Losing their soul. Losing their life.
Hand in hand. Husband and wife.
Up the aisle, down the path.
No turning back. Impending wrath.

No protection. Herds of the meek.
No limits of shame. Cowardly and weak.
Poisoned. Aflame. Maniacal prism.
Perish they will. Self-made cataclysm.

Piety, Royalty.
Curses of Humanity

World bound to Religion. World bound to Royalty.
Man's biggest monuments to blind loyalty.
Kings, Queens, Ministers of vandal.
Sanctuaries of nefarious scandal.

Be it that tired old monarchy.
With its nepotistic hierarchy.
Be it Eastern Buddhism.
Be it Neo-Judaism.
Be it the evil prism.
That is Roman Catholicism.
Her Majesty's cold-hearted flatlines.
The Roman Catholic's Nazi Ratlines.

Self-serving pontiffs of endless greed.
Parishioners fulfilling their every need.
B. C. or A. D., the same malaise.
Undeterred, in their cultish ways.

Resplendent in the finest robes and smocks.
Doing as they wish, to the unquestioning flocks.
Conspiring with verses. Prehistoric reflection.
Palms thrust open. Tithes of collection.

Monthly stipend, they come to expect.
Be you wealthy or indigent, they gladly accept.
Beware the crown. Beware the collar.
Without compunction, be it your very last dollar.
Never asked of possession or how they bought it.
Tax-free conglomerates, free of audit.

Buckingham Palace, the Vatican, whatever the Temple.
Requisitions, rather quite simple.
To these duties, they never refrain.
Unabashed. Receiving each ill-gotten gain.

Bless his Holiness? God save the Queen?
One would be shocked, if they ever came clean.
Her nauseating wave. His knowing nods.
Both born human, never Gods.

Unworthy. Deify them not.
Bedamned. The entire lot!

The Atomic Bomb that was Vietnam (Circa 1970)

Vietnam, a blind commission.
Perpetrated, a leaderless Panzer division.
Families are shrinking, nations are weeping.
Brothers are dying, while L.B.J.'s sleeping.
Five-star generals scratching their heads.
They won't lay down where they made their beds.

Troops misguided, a non-stop bungle.
V.C. creeping, their turf, their jungle.
Blood-stained warriors knee-deep in plasma.
Unable to see through the thick miasma.
Tough luck if your boy's a late bloomer.
Home in a box for the ex-baby boomer.

Night watch, no time to crash.
Daybreak light up from the stash.
Cold feet, temperature's risin'.
Napalm burns a new horizon.

Unseen enemy? The term applies.
Undetected, the company fries.
Club P.O.W., the cover charge doom.
Members only in the V.I.P. room.
Deadly villagers, incognito.

Friend or foe damn the torpedo!
D.M.Z.'s and M.I.A.'s.
Same ol', same ol', for a thousand days.
Mere kids playing the land mine game.
Each step could make you a lame.
Constant shelling, it ain't thunder.
This storm? Put you six feet under.

Media over hype? 6 O'clock news thriller.
Now they call your son "baby killer".
When he left home, we were so proud.
He returned to a U.S.A. wrapped in a shroud.
When they send you home? How they gonna mail ya'?
First-class stiff or third-class failure!

Punks in the Streets

The maniacal few and the harm they do.
Wound so tightly, turning the screw.
Driving a split, an irreversible wedge.
Self-serving radicals, always on edge.
Venom spewing forth, they scream and shout.
Faces aged by vitriol and doubt.

Raging torrents of misguided hate.
Minds closed at reason's gate.
If opened, possible path to revision.
Alas impeded, by myopic vision.

Always foreboding. Weapon-toting.
Purveyors of mayhem. Self-imploding.
Comical clowns, within a circus tent.
Reveling in chaos. Poison they vent.

Coast to coast. New York to Seattle.
The war they wage. A needless battle.
Contagious, rat-infested, blood sucking fleas.
Lame-ass radicals, rampant with disease.
Simple anarchists, they dream of revolution.
They have no plan. They seek no solution.

Society's dropouts, always so pissed.
Masked cowards. Girls in their midst.
Neurotic sisters. Emotional wrecks.
Back to the suburbs, with your cellphone and texts.
Nothing special. Modern-day hellion.
White collar thugs bent on rebellion.

Bitch and moan with all you might.
Your days are over. Good riddance. Good night.
Sit at Starbucks, tell the barista: "More latte in my cup."
Better yet, just stay home and shut the hell up!!

Mixed Heritage. Mixed Emotion

The Native American deserves utmost admiration.
Innocents. Victims of European conflagration.
Brutally evicted from their much-revered land.
Branded inferior, by Manifest Destiny's cruel hand.

Intentionally diseased. Infected. No immunities.
Race intent on genocide of the red man's communities.
White man's penchant to pillage and deceive.
Imprisoning spirituality. They could never conceive.

The blood of each flows through my veins.
Descendant torn. Ancestral pains.
I, with a love of nature's beings, big and small.
With shame, reluctance, I must recall.

Time and death healing a despicable lesion.
Wounds fading, by the slow elixir of reason.
Somewhat forgiven. Can the white man make amends?
Can the red man truly consider them friends?

The heavens, the sky, let us humbly beseech.
From each race, may we learn, may we teach.
One man cannot atone for sins of the father, sins of the past.
Perhaps a legacy of acceptance, a destiny of hope, that will
last.

Deathland? Deutschland!

Adolph Hitler, leader of the Third Reich.
Along with his henchmen and others of the like.
If living today? They'd be losers, geeks.
Paranoid midgets. Circus freaks!
Herr Hitler, Herr Himmler, Herr Hess, Herr Goebbels.
Pygmies on the hamster wheel, a clan of gerbils.

The only with an ounce of daring.
Baron von Fatman, Hermann Goering.
Clowns laughable, without humor.
Walking filth, a cancerous tumor.
Subterranean moles, they knew no depth.
Making deals with the devil. Pacts with death!
Keepers of the occult, dolts of Black Magic.
They would be funny, were they not so tragic!

A willing populace jumping through hoops.
With ringmasters nothing but nincompoops.
Which were the bigger fools?
The followers of course, led by spineless ghouls.
How do you measure such shame?
Maybe size XL? Extra lame?

For your sins, you shall never atone.
History deems you stand alone!

Your acts beyond redemption.
Willing cohorts, without exemption.
Make amends in some future generation.
Then, maybe, a return of some veneration.

For today's Nazi, a place in Hell.
The bastard's Inferno. Long may you dwell!

Nazis…cursed be thy name.
Suicidal cowards of ignominious fame.
Laboratory rats. Lost in an inescapable maze.
May you incinerate, into the infernal blaze.

The Battered Woman Syndrome?

The battered woman. Queen of self-sabotage.
Where there is reality, she sees a mirage.
When choosing a mate, she seems so confused.
Time after time, she returns, to be the abused.

With children in tow, she can't walk away.
Endangering all, she chooses to stay.
She has the power; she has a voice.
It is not a syndrome; it is a choice.

Imprisoned by the shackles of doubt.
The key within reach, if she would simply get out!
Blindly accepting. Never rejecting. Losing her soul.
The monster she lays down with, in total control.

Forgoing the concept of simple common sense.
She is a danger. Beyond recompense!

Stars and Bars.
Remove the Scars

It is high time to remove all scars.
Blanche white, stains of the Stars and Bars.
These blemishes remain eternal.
Memories in Hell. War infernal.
Battles of bloodshed and bravery.
All in the name of wretched slavery.

Black mark to Dixie, may you always carry.
Robert E. Lee, head mercenary.
Caring not of nation or damage done.
Nothing more than rebel hired gun.
General in uniform. Striking and gallant.
Selling his soul. Abuse of talent.

Soldiers committed to cause of separation.
Prisoners bound. To leaders of desperation.
Wake of destruction. Farm and city.
Army incapable of shame or pity.
Subservient to plantational whim.
Mindless beasts. Losing life and limb.

View them not with an ounce of kindness.
Curse them and their superior blindness.
May we remember as long as we live.

To never forget. To never forgive.
Reasons and actions, you cannot defend.
May the South never rise again!

Thoughts of Reflection through Quiet Contemplation

- "Notoriety and serenity cannot coexist. Thunder must crash! Lightning must flash! Be a force of nature and get noticed!"

- "A child's quest for knowledge should never be trivialized. A question asked, give it undivided attention." –

- "If one must dream. Dream big! Otherwise, go back to sleep." –

- "At present, the disease of distance infects us all…The truest tragedy has come to call." –

- "This imposed solitude has offered each of us mirrored moments of self-reflection. Do you like what you see?"

- "The human brain is like a light bulb. It can burn brightly with the glow of discovery. It will flicker with self-deception or burn out with evil thoughts and deeds. Be not a light bulb. Be the Sun! First, absorb the power. Then, dispense the power!" –

- "A man's soul is where his character and conscience reside. Does he like living there?" –

- "Is man not allowed to question those Almighty? Damned right he is!" –

- "So hard to find a hero in such a non-heroic time. Even the most magnificent find it difficult to make their mark." –
- "If religion were logical, it would be science."-
- "The harshest reality in life is a dream denied." –

- "To be ignorant of sophistication and class. Is not to have it!" –

- "Intimacy is made for two. Sacred moments that should never be shared with others. Speak of it only in general terms. No names involved." –

- "The deeds of men can be so foul. They deserve neither the hand of forgiveness, nor the gift of redemption." –
- "Never waste pity on those of great stupidity."

- "Man's craving and lust for enlightenment should be his greatest addiction. He must abuse it." –

- "Violence is but temporary insanity…Personified!"

- "At times man is but a step above the hyena. In only the fact we don't consume each other." –

- "The value of advice is only worth the value of those receiving it." –

- "One's true greatness can be as limitless as the Giant Redwood. With patience, inspiration and understanding it will take root and soar to the heavens." –

- "Wisdom is much easier imparted, than applied." –
- "Allow the divine omnipotence of nature to engulf and empower your very being to the core!" –

- "No man's death or demise is insignificant. A soul lost. A monument of waste. Human tragedy." –